# ARGYLL and the HIGHLANDS' LAST DAYS OF STEAM

*by*
W.A.C. Smith

Class K2 2-6-0 No. 61776 runs into Helensburgh Upper Station, the locomotive crew are exchanging the token for single line working with the signalman, heading the Sunday 8.00 p.m. from Ardlui to Bridgeton Central on 15 July 1956. This train was run to obviate overcrowding on the regular Fort William excursion.

ISBN 1 84033 317 0

**The publishers regret that they cannot supply
copies of any pictures featured in this book.**

Class K2 2-6-6 No. 61776 again and seen here leaving Shandon station high above the Gareloch hauling the 3.00 p.m. from Glasgow Queen Street to Ardlui on 1 September 1956. The station at Shandon was closed in 1964 and little remains.

# INTRODUCTION

Argyll may seem an unlikely venue for railway building, but during the railway mania of 1845 speculative schemes proliferated. None, however, came to fruition until 1865 when the Callander & Oban Railway obtained an Act for a railway between those places. The railway connected with the existing Dunblane, Doune & Callander and reached Stirling over the lines of the Scottish Central (later the Caledonian) Railway. The new line reached Killin (Glenoglehead) in 1870, Tyndrum in 1873, Dalmally in 1877 and Oban in 1880, being worked by the Caledonian although it remained nominally independent until 1923, and the government inspired grouping. The Killin branch was opened in 1886 and the Ballachulish branch was opened in 1903.

Some two years after completion of the Callander & Oban the Glasgow & North Western Railway was promoted to run from Glasgow to Inverness. It would have run along the east side of Loch Lomond, Crianlarich (with a link to the Oban line), Glencoe, Fort William and through the Great Glen to Inverness. In spite of substantial backing its Parliamentary Bill was defeated in 1883.

In 1889 the West Highland Railway Act was passed, authorising a line from Fort William via Rannoch Moor, Tyndrum, Crianlarich (again with a link to the Callander & Oban), Glen Falloch and the west side of Loch Lomond to a junction with the North British Railway at Craigendoran. It was opened in 1894 and an extension to Mallaig followed in 1901. The West Highland Railway was absorbed by the North British Railway in 1908.

From Spean Bridge on the West Highland line the Invergarry & Fort Augustus Railway was opened in 1903 and had a troubled history. Initially it was worked by the Highland Railway, who viewed it as a potential threat to their monopoly of Inverness traffic. The North British Railway took over the line in 1907 and operated it until 1911 when they shut it down for two years owing to losses incurred, the NBR resumed operation in 1913. The passenger traffic was ended by the London and North Eastern in 1933 and a meagre freight service survived until 1946.

The Highland Railway was created in 1865 by the amalgamation of the Inverness & Aberdeen Junction Railway and the Inverness & Perth Junction Railway. The Dingwall & Skye Railway was opened in 1870, being extended to Kyle of Lochalsh in 1897. The route north to Wick and Thurso was completed in 1874 although the several companies formed to complete the line remained independent for a further ten years. The costly Aviemore to Inverness direct line via Carr Bridge was finally completed in 1898, having been put forward previously to block the proposed Glasgow & North Western Railway.

The precarious financial position of the country's railways following the First World War brought about the Government inspired Railway Grouping of 1923 with the formation of four large companies: London Midland & Scottish (LMS); London & North Eastern (LNER); Great Western (GWR) and Southern (SR). The inter-war years saw an imaginative campaign by the 'Big Four' to regain lost traffic. In Argyll and the Highlands innovations included cheap day and evening fares, restaurant cars, Sunday excursions, circular tours by train and ship, and camping coaches, augmented during the British Railways era by observation cars, Television Train excursions and the Six Lochs Diesel Land Cruise.

Such initiatives are sadly lacking on today's Scotrail. However, to sell travel by noisy, draughty, outdated diesel multiple units cluttered with backpackers and their impediments and with viewing of the often spectacular scenery severely restricted by the uncontrolled growth of lineside vegetation, is undoubtably beset with difficulties. The holding out of the begging bowl to be filled by an indulgent taxpayer is an ever so much easier option.

Dr Beeching's report into the reshaping of the nationalised British Railways, published in 1963, recommended closing half of the existing 17,000 miles of track together with 2,000 stations, phasing out of steam traction and the introduction of freighliner services. The report brought closure to part of the original Highland main line, from Aviemore to Forres via Dava in the autumn of 1965. The Callander & Oban line between Dunblane and Crianlarich, including the Killin branch, was also closed that autumn, and resulted in the diversion of Oban trains to the West Highland line. The Ballachulish branch was abandoned in the spring of 1966.

During 1962 steam locomotives were replaced by diesels on these lines, with exception of Killin and a few Stirling to Callander workings. When the Killin branch was closed prematurely on Monday, 27 September 1965, together with the line from Callander to Crianlarich, because of a rock fall in Glen Ogle, the locomotive in use was standard 2-6-4T No. 80093. The Dunblane to Callander section was closed as planned on Monday, 1 November 1965, the last steam train being the 5.50 p.m. from Glasgow Buchanan Street to Callander on Saturday, 30 October worked by Black Five No. 45396.

On a happier note, 2004 marks twenty one years of a steam hauled passenger service during the summer months between Fort William and Mallaig. The service was begun by British Rail in 1984 and is currently operated by the West Coast Railway Co. of Carnforth in Lancashire. Preserved locomotives are used for the train, originally named 'The Lochaber' but now called 'The Jacobite', and have included various Black Fives, class 8F 2-8-0 No. 48151, standard class 4 No. 75014, B1 4-6-0 No. 61264 and K1 No. 62005.

On 24 September 1956, Black Five 4-6-0 No. 44908 pauses at Ardlui with an 8.50 a.m. 'Evening Citizen Television Show Train' from Glasgow Queen Street to Oban. This was the inaugural outing for the Scottish Region's newly created TV train and it was run in two portions with the second train hauled by Black Five No. 44956.

In brilliant sunshine, and having made an excellent run to regain several minutes of lost time despite having a six coach train 'full and standing' in railway parlance, class D34 4-4-0 No. 62496 'Glen Loy' shunts the empty stock of the new Saturday's only 3.00 p.m. from Glasgow Queen Street to Ardlui on 23 July 1955 (in later years the train was extended to Crianlarich Upper) which provided a popular 'Loch Lomond Circular Tour', at a cost of five shillings and sixpence, with passengers sailing down the loch to Balloch for a return train service to Glasgow. Unfortunately, closure of Ardlui pier in 1964 brought this to an end.

Paddle steamer *Maid of the Loch* at Ardlui on 23 July 1955, for 6.30 p.m. sailing to Balloch. Built at the Glasgow shipyard of A & J Inglis she was dismantled and transported in sections by rail to Balloch to be reconstructed on the loch side and entered service on 25 May 1953. After changes in ownership, and dwindling passenger numbers, she sailed for the last time on 30 August 1981, and was laid up at Balloch where she remains. She is currently undergoing restoration by The *Maid of the Loch* Trust and The Loch Lomond Steamship Company for a possible return to service.

Class K4 2-6-0 No. 61995 'Cameron of Lochiel' at Crianlarich Upper with a Stephenson Locomotive Society railtour returning from Fort William to Glasgow on 18 June 1960. The K4s had been specially designed for the West Highland route in 1937, and this was the last occasion on which one worked over the line.

At Crianlarich Upper on 20 June 1959 Black Five Nos. 44975 and 44956 arrive with the 5.05 p.m. train from Fort William to Glasgow Queen Street while class K2 2-6-0 No. 61787 'Loch Quoich' waits to work the 8.00 p.m. train to Glasgow. The K2s had a reputation for rough riding and I found this to be more than justified when the driver kindly offered me a footplate trip. Nevertheless, when 'Loch Quoich' went for scrap later that year I purchased (for the princely sum of £5) one of its brass nameplates as a memento.

Class K2 2-6-0 No. 61786 and B1 4-6-0 No. 61261 use the connecting spur at Crianlarich with a 1.45 p.m. Television Train excursion from Glasgow Buchanan Street returning to Glasgow Queen Street on 20 June 1959.

On 1 June 1963, preserved North British Railway 4-4-0 No. 256 'Glen Douglas' and class J37 0-6-0 No. 64632 double headed the Scottish Locomotive Preservation Fund 'Jacobite' railtour leaving Glasgow Queen Street at 7.53 a.m. for Fort William and Mallaig and seen in this photograph at Bridge of Orchy. Unfortunately, the J37 had soon to be detached because of overheating bearings and 'Glen Douglas' despite assistance from a diesel locomotive failed upon arrival at Fort William. A pair of J37s took over here, but upon arrival at Mallaig (2½ hours late) one was declared a failure and the return journey was made behind a diesel locomotive to reach Glasgow some two hours late shortly after midnight. All in all, a not uneventful journey for what had been billed as a 'Last Steam Train on the West Highland'! Fortunately, the weather remained fine throughout.

Black Five 4-6-0s Nos. 44921 and 44973 upon arrival at Fort William on 5 September 1954, punctually at 2.23 p.m. with the 9.45 a.m. Sunday excursion from Bridgeton Central carrying some 300 passengers and loaded to nine coaches including restaurant car. The latter, selling copious amounts of liquid refreshments played no small part in the popularity of these trains which had been introduced by the London and North Eastern Railway in the 1930s. After the Second World War they were restored by British Railways, at a fare of fifteen shillings return, but fell victim to an economy drive in 1958.

Veteran class J36 0-6-0 No. 65313, built by the North British Railway in 1899, shunts empty coaching stock out of the old Fort William terminus on 18 June 1960. This was replaced in 1975 by a new station, inconveniently situated some distance from the town centre, to allow for a road improvement scheme.

Class K2 2-6-0 No. 61764 'Loch Arkaig' at Fort William motive power depot on 5 September 1954. The K2s were a Great Northern Railway design dating back to 1914 and chiefly intended for freight work. Following upon the railway grouping fourteen were transferred to Scotland in 1925, initially to cope with the increasing weight of trains on the West Highland Line, being joined by a further six in 1932 and reaching a total of thirty in 1951. They were fitted with side window cabs in view of what was described as Scotland's inclement weather, and thirteen received the names of West Highland lochs. By 1961 only 'Loch Arkaig' remained in service and I arranged for it to make a farewell trip to Crianlarich in June of that year.

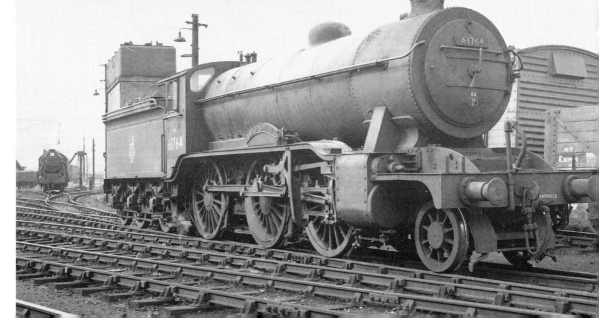

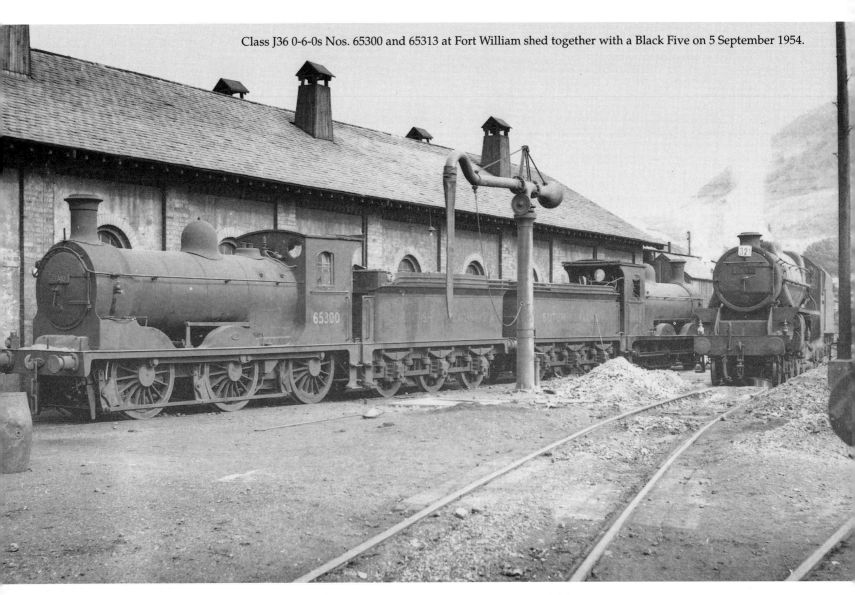

Class J36 0-6-0s Nos. 65300 and 65313 at Fort William shed together with a Black Five on 5 September 1954.

Class K2 2-6-0 No. 61784 takes water at Glenfinnan station on 21 July 1958 with the 2.45 p.m. train from Mallaig to Fort William and Glasgow.

Class K2 2-6-0s Nos. 61784 and 61764 'Loch Arkaig' leave Glenfinnan half an hour late with the heavily loaded 5.15 a.m. Glasgow Queen Street to Mallaig on Glasgow Fair Monday 21 July 1958, having taken over the train at Fort William where reversal is required.

Class K1 2-6-0 No. 62012 shunting at Mallaig, the end of the line, on 21 July 1958 when the terminus possessed platform canopies. Regrettably these were removed some twenty years later.

Now we move to the Callander and Oban Line. On 6 August, 1960 Black Five No. 45470 arrives at Dunblane, 45 minutes late, with the 5.15 p.m. from Glasgow Buchanan Street to Oban. Class B1 4-6-0 No. 61067, seen on the right, had worked the 5.35 p.m. local train from Buchanan Street and was pressed into service to assist the ailing No. 45470.

Preserved Caledonian Railway 4-2-2 No. 123 paired with two restored coaches and forming a Stephenson Locomotive Society railtour from Glasgow Buchanan Street leaves Doune for Callander on 10 October 1964.

Situated between Doune and Callander was a crossing loop at Drumvaich and Black Five No. 45359 is seen passing with the 1.18 p.m. from Callander to Glasgow Buchanan Street on 11 September 1965.

A view of Callander station from the east. Class 4 2-6-4T No. 42199 awaits departure with the 5.45 p.m. train for Stirling on 21 August 1954. A car park now occupies the station site.

A busy scene at Callander on Easter Monday, 30 March 1959. A 'Six Lochs Diesel Land Cruise' from Glasgow Buchanan Street returning to Glasgow Queen Street stands at the main arrival platform. Next to it is Black Five No. 45153 heading the 9.18 a.m. from Oban to Glasgow and No. 45213 is on an up freight while a horse box occupies the dock platform. Also present was B1 No. 61349 which had worked the 11.12 a.m. from Stirling.

Black Five No. 45214 skirts Loch Lubnaig with the 12.45 p.m. summer Saturday's train from Oban to Edinburgh Princes Street on 12 August 1961. In winter the through coaches from Oban to Edinburgh were conveyed to Stirling by the Glasgow bound train. Note the beautiful condition of the track.

With a good head of steam for the 1 in 60 climb to Glenoglehead Black Five No. 45496 passes Strathyre with the 11.50 a.m. express from Glasgow to Oban on 12 August 1961. This formed a relief to the 12.00 noon service in the days when workers were restricted to a two week annual break and travelled in large numbers at summer weekends to holiday destinations.

Preserved Caledonian locomotive 4-2-2 No. 123 and North British Railway 4-4-0 No. 256 'Glen Douglas' pass Glenoglehead crossing place with a Stephenson Locomotive Society special returning from Oban to Glasgow Buchanan Street on 12 May 1962. At 941 ft. Glenoglehead (Queen Victoria's Khyber Pass of Scotland) was the summit of the Callander and Oban line, its temporary terminus for three years and the original station for Killin. It was here that a minor rock fall, in September 1965, resulted in premature closure of the line.

Caledonian Railway No. 123 at Killin Junction in blizzard conditions with the 'Scottish Rambler No. 2' railtour from Glasgow Central to Crianlarich, return being by way of the West Highland line, on 12 April 1963. Type 2 diesel locomotives Nos. D5354 and D5348 are running in (15 minutes late) with the 12.05 p.m. from Oban to Glasgow Buchanan Street. The popular 'Scottish Rambler' railtours were promoted jointly by the Branch Line Society and the Stephenson Locomotive Society and ran annually at Easter weekend from 1962 to the end of steam in 1968.

On the fine, sunny evening of 18 June 1960, Black Five No 45125 passes Killin Junction with the 5.15 p.m. Glasgow Buchanan Street to Oban. The five mile Killin branch drops on a gradient of 1 in 50 behind the signal box.

The Killin branch train service originally ran to Loch Tay station, connecting with steamer services on the loch, but the last mile of the branch was closed to passengers upon outbreak of war in 1939 although it continued to be used by the branch locomotive working to its small shed on the loch side. The station building survived as a private residence, and standard 2-6-4T No. 80092 is seen here on 18 June 1962 with a 'Scottish Tour' special for railway enthusiasts from south of the border.

Preserved Great North of Scotland Railway 4-4-0 No. 49 'Gordon Highlander' visited Oban on 14 May 1960 with a Glasgow University special originating at Glasgow Queen Street and seen here in the Pass of Brander, on its return journey to Glasgow Buchanan Street. It is passing one of the automatic stone signals which went to danger if a boulder from the steep hillside fell and broke the line side fencing to land on the track.

Preserved GNSR No. 49 is seen earlier on its return journey with the Glasgow University special climbing the 1 in 50 Glencruitten bank out of Oban. The train consisted of the two restored Caledonian Railway Coaches and a former Pullman observation car.

Preserved CR No. 123 and NBR No. 256 make a smoky exit from Oban with the Stephenson Locomotive Society special of 12 May 1962, bound for Glasgow Buchanan Street. The outward journey, starting from Glasgow Central, had been over the West Highland line to Crianlarich where the Oban line was joined.

As previously mentioned (page 4) the TV train had its first outing on 24 September 1956 to Oban where the two portions of the train were photographed, headed by Black Five Nos. 44908 and 44956 respectively, awaiting departure for Glasgow Buchanan Street. In the event No. 44908 slipped to a stand on Glencruitten bank and had to be banked to the summit by another Black Five, No. 44967, off a freight train. During the afternoon two public showings had been held in the trains and proved popular as Oban had no television reception at that time. Oban's station facilities were 'rationalised' in 1985 resulting in a minimum of sheltered accommodation for passengers in the not infrequent event of wet weather.

The 27¾ mile Ballachulish branch diverged from the Oban line 6¼ miles out at Connel Ferry and of its four trains (five on Saturdays) one started from the junction station, the others being through from Oban. One of the latter, the well filled 4.55 p.m. school train, is seen departing on 24 September 1956 hauled by class 2P 0-4-4T No. 55200. These former Caledonian Railway locomotives monopolised the Ballachulish branch for most of its sixty three years and another of the class No. 55208 is seen on the left acting as Oban station pilot.

The Connel Ferry bridge was a notable engineering feature on the Ballachulish branch and carried the railway and a single track roadway, on which a toll was levied, across the Falls of Lora at the mouth of Loch Etive. On 14 May 1960 class 2P 0-4-4T No. 55224 was photographed coming off the bridge with the 3.47 p.m. train from Ballachulish. Today the bridge remains in use for road traffic.

Ballachulish Ferry station adjoined the ferry across Loch Leven and is seen on 26 May 1958 with class 2P 0-4-4T No. 55208 heading the 3.48 p.m. from Ballachulish to Oban. Both the railway and ferry are long gone, the latter replaced by a road bridge in 1975.

Ballachulish, station for Glencoe and Kinlochleven as the branch terminal was officially known, lay in the shadow of the famous slate quarries and was photographed on 19 July 1954, with class 2P 0-4-4T No. 55195 heading the 3.55 p.m. train for Oban.

Grandiose nineteenth century plans for railways from Ballachulish to Fort William and Inverness came to nothing, but photographically we are enabled to join the former Highland Railway at Dalnaspidal seen on 15 June 1960, with preserved Highland Railway 4-6-0 No. 103 passing through south bound with a six day 'Scottish Railtour' for enthusiasts, starting from Edinburgh and finishing at Glasgow it got as far north as Aberdeen and Inverness, and which, as Scottish Area Secretary of the Stephenson Locomotive Society, I helped organise.

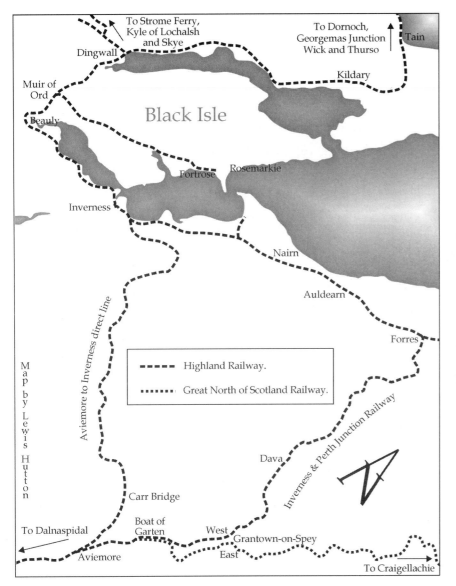

Map by Lewis Hutton

To Strome Ferry, Kyle of Lochalsh and Skye

Dingwall

To Dornoch, Georgemas Junction Wick and Thurso

Tain

Muir of Ord

Black Isle

Kildary

Beauly

Rosemarkie

Fortrose

Inverness

Nairn

Auldearn

Aviemore to Inverness direct line

Forres

- - - - Highland Railway.

········ Great North of Scotland Railway.

Inverness & Perth Junction Railway

Dava

Carr Bridge

Boat of Garten

West

To Dalnaspidal

Grantown-on-Spey

East

Aviemore

To Craigellachie

Proceeding north we reach Aviemore from where the original Highland main line ran via Boat of Garten and Grantown-on-Spey to Forres and thence Inverness. Boat of Garten was served also by the Great North of Scotland Railway from Craigellachie and on 31 August 1955, class 3F former Caledonian Railway 0-6-0 No. 57634 is about to depart from 'the Boat' with the 1.00 p.m. train along the Speyside line to Craigellachie. Fifty years later and, hopefully, the scene will come back when preserved Caledonian Railway 0-6-0 No. 828, currently under overhaul at Aviemore, returns to service on the Strathspey Railway.

Another view at Boat of Garten, on 31 August 1955, with Black Five No. 45136 passing on the former Highland line with a southbound freight train. Closed by British Railways in 1965 the line was reopened as far as Boat of Garten in 1978 by the enthusiast inspired Strathspey Railway which has reached Broomhill and has Grantown-on-Spey as its long term objective.

Grantown-on-Spey had in fact two stations. The East station was on the Craigellachie line and closed in 1968, and is seen on 28 August 1959, with class 3F 0-6-0 No. 57634 in the loop with a freight and waiting to cross a diesel railbus bound for Elgin.

Grantown-on-Spey (West) station on the Highland line was a more pretentious affair as befitted a main line and Black Five No. 44698 was photographed on 28 August 1959 taking water while working the 10.10 a.m. train from Inverness to Glasgow Buchanan Street. Following its closure the station was razed to the ground.

At Forres there was a triangular junction with the line from Aberdeen to Inverness. In this view taken on 14 June 1960, class 2P 4-4-0 No. 40663 is standing on the south to west side of the triangle with the previously mentioned 'Scottish Railtour' train.

Auldearn station, situated between Forres and Nairn, was closed in 1960. On 16 June 1962, Black Five No. 44978 passes by en route from Inverness to Aviemore with a 'Scottish Railtour' special train.

Inverness station was (and is) a curious affair, being a terminus with a short all over roof, narrow, curving platforms and situated at the apex of a triangle formed by the north and south lines respectively with the base of the triangle consisting of a connecting line known as the Rose Street curve which, in the days of steam, was used to reverse trains into the station. On 31 August 1955, Black Five No. 44703 and B1 No. 61323 await departure with the 7.40 a.m. train for Aberdeen.

Inverness motive power depot comprised a semi circular shed housing some fifty locomotives and had its own peculiarity in the shape of a smoke blackened stone arch, carrying a 45,000 gallon water tank. Seen straddling the approach tracks in the background, left, of this photograph taken in August 1955, which also shows former Caledonian Railway 4-4-0 No. 54463 and 0-6-0T No. 56291.

Black Five No. 45461 runs into Beauly station with the 10.40 a.m. train from Inverness to Wick on 27 August 1959 having covered the first ten miles of its 161½ mile northbound journey.

Muir of Ord, three miles beyond Beauly, was junction for the 13½ mile Black Isle branch. On 25 August 1959, Black Five No. 45478 calls at Muir of Ord with the 12.05 p.m. local service from Tain to Inverness.

In this view at the north end of Muir of Ord on 25 August 1959, Black Five No. 45461 is entering the station with the 3.45 p.m. train from Tain to Inverness while former Caledonian Railway 0-6-0 No. 57594 stands on the Fortrose branch seen curving away behind the passenger train.

The local service of two or three trains between Tain and Inverness was frequently worked by former Caledonian Railway 4-4-0s as on 27 August 1959 when No. 54470 was photographed coming off the single line at small Kildary station with the 12.05 p.m. from Tain while Black Five No. 45461 waits in the passing loop with the 10.40 a.m. from Inverness to Wick. The station master has boxes of flowers for Forres, the local postman has bags of mail for Inverness and there are three prospective passengers.

Black Five No. 45461 takes water at Tain while working the 10.40 a.m. train from Inverness to Wick the leading vehicle of which is a former Highland Railway travelling post office van. 27 August 1959.

From the curiously named station of The Mound, the name came from the causeway built by Thomas Telford to carry a road across the head of Loch Fleet, a 7¾ mile branch was opened in 1902 to the county town of Dornoch where a large hotel was built by the Highland Railway which is reputed to have cost more than the railway! The branch was worked under a light railway order which restricted the axle loading of the locomotives. When in 1956, the sole surviving Highland Railway locomotive in normal service broke a driving axle on the branch, it was replaced by a pair of Western Region 0-6-0 pannier tanks one of which, No. 1649, is seen shunting at Dornoch on 27 August 1959. The branch was closed in 1960.

The Far North line forks at Georgemas Junction to serve Wick and Thurso respectively, these being the furthest north stations on the rail network, and on 24 August 1959 Black Five 4-6-0s Nos. 44789 and 44783 were about to depart from Wick with the 3.35 p.m. to Inverness.